2019

AMAZING
Grace

16-MONTH WEEKLY PLANNER

BELLE CITY GIFTS

SEPTEMBER 2018	OCTOBER 2018	NOVEMBER 2018	DECEMBER 2018
S M T W T F S	S M T W T F S	S M T W T F S	S M T W T F S
1	1 2 3 4 5 6	1 2 3	1
2 3 4 5 6 7 8	7 8 9 10 11 12 13	4 5 6 7 8 9 10	2 3 4 5 6 7 8
9 10 11 12 13 14 15	14 15 16 17 18 19 20	11 12 13 14 15 16 17	9 10 11 12 13 14 15
16 17 18 19 20 21 22	21 22 23 24 25 26 27	18 19 20 21 22 23 24	16 17 18 19 20 21 22
23 24 25 26 27 28 29	28 29 30 31	25 26 27 28 29 30	23 24 25 26 27 28 29
30			30 31

JANUARY 2019	FEBRUARY 2019	MARCH 2019	APRIL 2019
S M T W T F S	S M T W T F S	S M T W T F S	S M T W T F S
1 2 3 4 5	1 2	1 2	1 2 3 4 5 6
6 7 8 9 10 11 12	3 4 5 6 7 8 9	3 4 5 6 7 8 9	7 8 9 10 11 12 13
13 14 15 16 17 18 19	10 11 12 13 14 15 16	10 11 12 13 14 15 16	14 15 16 17 18 19 20
20 21 22 23 24 25 26	17 18 19 20 21 22 23	17 18 19 20 21 22 23	21 22 23 24 25 26 27
27 28 29 30 31	24 25 26 27 28	24 25 26 27 28 29 30	28 29 30
		31	

MAY 2019	JUNE 2019	JULY 2019	AUGUST 2019
S M T W T F S	S M T W T F S	S M T W T F S	S M T W T F S
1 2 3 4	1	1 2 3 4 5 6	1 2 3
5 6 7 8 9 10 11	2 3 4 5 6 7 8	7 8 9 10 11 12 13	4 5 6 7 8 9 10
12 13 14 15 16 17 18	9 10 11 12 13 14 15	14 15 16 17 18 19 20	11 12 13 14 15 16 17
19 20 21 22 23 24 25	16 17 18 19 20 21 22	21 22 23 24 25 26 27	18 19 20 21 22 23 24
26 27 28 29 30 31	23 24 25 26 27 28 29	28 29 30 31	25 26 27 28 29 30 31
	30		

SEPTEMBER 2019	OCTOBER 2019	NOVEMBER 2019	DECEMBER 2019
S M T W T F S	S M T W T F S	S M T W T F S	S M T W T F S
1 2 3 4 5 6 7	1 2 3 4 5	1 2	1 2 3 4 5 6 7
8 9 10 11 12 13 14	6 7 8 9 10 11 12	3 4 5 6 7 8 9	8 9 10 11 12 13 14
15 16 17 18 19 20 21	13 14 15 16 17 18 19	10 11 12 13 14 15 16	15 16 17 18 19 20 21
22 23 24 25 26 27 28	20 21 22 23 24 25 26	17 18 19 20 21 22 23	22 23 24 25 26 27 28
29 30	27 28 29 30 31	24 25 26 27 28 29 30	29 30 31

Introduction

Having trouble fitting everything in your day? This 16-month planner makes getting organized simple and inspiring.

Each beautifully designed page blends practical weekly plans with motivating Scripture. High-quality paper allows you to confidently write reminders, schedules, and personal notes in the space provided.

Stay organized and be encouraged as you plan each day with *Amazing Grace.*

September
2018

One thing I have desired of the LORD,

That will I seek:

That I may dwell in the house of the LORD

All the days of my life,

To behold the beauty of the LORD

And to inquire in His temple.

PSALM 27:4 NKJV

S	M	T	W	T	F	S
						1
2	3	4	5	6	7	8
9	10	11	12	13	14	15
16	17	18	19	20	21	22
23	24	25	26	27	28	29
30						

August / September

27 Monday

_____
_____
_____
_____

28 Tuesday

_____
_____
_____
_____

29 Wednesday

_____
_____
_____
_____

_____

_____

_____

_____

_____

Friday 31

_____

_____

_____

_____

_____

Saturday 1

_____

_____

_____

Sunday 2

_____

_____

_____

THE LORD WILL GIVE STRENGTH TO HIS PEOPLE;
THE LORD WILL BLESS HIS PEOPLE WITH PEACE.

Psalm 29:11 NKJV

September

3 Monday LABOR DAY

_____
_____
_____
_____
_____

4 Tuesday

_____
_____
_____
_____
_____

5 Wednesday

_____
_____
_____
_____
_____

Thursday 6

Friday 7

Saturday 8

Sunday 9

BLESSED IS ANYONE WHO ENDURES TEMPTATION.
SUCH A ONE HAS STOOD THE TEST AND WILL RECEIVE
THE CROWN OF LIFE THAT THE LORD HAS PROMISED
TO THOSE WHO LOVE HIM.

James 1:12 NRSV

September

10 Monday   ROSH HASHANAH

_____

_____

_____

_____

_____

11 Tuesday

_____

_____

_____

_____

_____

12 Wednesday

_____

_____

_____

_____

_____

_____
_____
_____
_____
_____

Friday 14

_____
_____
_____
_____
_____

Saturday 15

_____
_____
_____

Sunday 16

_____
_____
_____

My voice You shall hear in the morning, O Lord;
In the morning I will direct it to You,
And I will look up.

Psalm 5:3 NKJV

September

17 Monday

_____
_____
_____
_____
_____

18 Tuesday   YOM KIPPUR

_____
_____
_____
_____
_____

19 Wednesday

_____
_____
_____
_____
_____

Friday 21

Saturday 22

AUTUMNAL EQUINOX Sunday 23

THE LORD ALWAYS KEEPS HIS PROMISES;
HE IS GRACIOUS IN ALL HE DOES.

Psalm 145:13 NLT

September

24 Monday

_____
_____
_____
_____
_____

25 Tuesday

_____
_____
_____
_____
_____

26 Wednesday

_____
_____
_____
_____
_____

Thursday 27

Friday 28

Saturday 29

Sunday 30

YOUR PROMISES HAVE BEEN THOROUGHLY TESTED,
AND YOUR SERVANT LOVES THEM.

Psalm 119:40 NIV

October
2018

Be truly glad! There is wonderful joy ahead.... You love him even though you have never seen him. Though you do not see him now, you trust him; and you rejoice with a glorious, inexpressible joy.

1 PETER 1:6, 8–9 NLT

S	M	T	W	T	F	S
	1	2	3	4	5	6
7	8	9	10	11	12	13
14	15	16	17	18	19	20
21	22	23	24	25	26	27
28	29	30	31			

October

1 Monday

_____
_____
_____
_____
_____

2 Tuesday

_____
_____
_____
_____
_____

3 Wednesday

_____
_____
_____
_____
_____

Thursday 4

_____

_____

_____

_____

Friday 5

_____

_____

_____

_____

Saturday 6

_____

_____

Sunday 7

_____

_____

_____

THE DESIRES OF THE DILIGENT ARE FULLY SATISFIED.

Proverbs 13:4 NIV

October

8 Monday COLUMBUS DAY

_____

_____

_____

_____

_____

9 Tuesday

_____

_____

_____

_____

_____

10 Wednesday

_____

_____

_____

_____

_____

Thursday 11

Friday 12

Saturday 13

Sunday 14

He will give eternal life to those who
keep on doing good,
seeking after the glory and honor and
immortality that God offers.

Romans 2:7 NLT

October

15 Monday

_____
_____
_____
_____

16 Tuesday

_____
_____
_____
_____

17 Wednesday

_____
_____
_____
_____
_____

Thursday 18

Friday 19

Saturday 20

Sunday 21

My flesh and my heart may fail,
but God is the strength of my heart
and my portion forever.

Psalm 73:26 NIV

October

22 Monday

_____
_____
_____
_____

23 Tuesday

_____
_____
_____
_____

24 Wednesday

_____
_____
_____
_____
_____

Thursday 25

Friday 26

Saturday 27

Sunday 28

FOR YOU WHO FEAR MY NAME,
THE SUN OF RIGHTEOUSNESS SHALL RISE
WITH HEALING IN ITS WINGS.

Malachi 4:2 ESV

November
2018

Praise the Lord!

Praise God in his sanctuary;

praise him in his mighty heavens!

Praise him for his mighty deeds;

praise him according to his excellent greatness!

Let everything that has breath praise the Lord!

Praise the Lord!

PSALM 150:1-2, 6 ESV

S	M	T	W	T	F	S
				1	2	3
4	5	6	7	8	9	10
11	12	13	14	15	16	17
18	19	20	21	22	23	24
25	26	27	28	29	30	

October/November

29 Monday

_____
_____
_____
_____
_____

30 Tuesday

_____
_____
_____
_____
_____

31 Wednesday

_____
_____
_____
_____
_____

Thursday   1

_____

_____

_____

_____

_____

Friday   2

_____

_____

_____

_____

Saturday   3

_____

_____

_____

DAYLIGHT SAVING TIME ENDS   Sunday   4

_____

_____

_____

THOSE WHO KNOW YOUR NAME WILL PUT THEIR TRUST IN YOU;
FOR YOU, LORD, HAVE NOT FORSAKEN THOSE WHO SEEK YOU.

Psalm 9:10 NKJV

November

5   Monday

_____
_____
_____
_____

6   Tuesday

_____
_____
_____
_____

7   Wednesday

_____
_____
_____
_____
_____

Thursday 8

_____

_____

_____

_____

_____

Friday 9

_____

_____

_____

_____

Saturday 10

_____

_____

_____

VETERANS' DAY   Sunday 11

_____

_____

_____

I TRUST IN YOU, O LORD;
I SAY, "YOU ARE MY GOD."
MY TIMES ARE IN YOUR HAND.

Psalm 31:14-15 ESV

November

12 Monday

_____
_____
_____
_____
_____

13 Tuesday

_____
_____
_____
_____
_____

14 Wednesday

_____
_____
_____
_____
_____

Thursday 15

Friday 16

Saturday 17

Sunday 18

THE LAW OF THE LORD IS PERFECT,
REFRESHING THE SOUL.

Psalm 19:7 NIV

November

19 Monday

_____
_____
_____
_____
_____

20 Tuesday

_____
_____
_____
_____
_____

21 Wednesday

_____
_____
_____
_____
_____

_____

_____

_____

_____

_____

Friday 23

_____

_____

_____

_____

Saturday 24

_____

_____

_____

Sunday 25

_____

_____

_____

YOU WERE CLEANSED FROM YOUR SINS WHEN YOU OBEYED THE TRUTH.

1 Peter 1:22 NLT

November/December

26 Monday

_____
_____
_____
_____

27 Tuesday

_____
_____
_____
_____

28 Wednesday

_____
_____
_____
_____

Thursday 29

Friday 30

Saturday 1

Sunday 2

DO NOT LET WISDOM AND UNDERSTANDING OUT OF YOUR SIGHT,
PRESERVE SOUND JUDGMENT AND DISCRETION;
THEY WILL BE LIFE FOR YOU.

Proverbs 3:21-22 NIV

December
2018

O LORD, You have searched me and known me.

You know my sitting down and my rising up;

You understand my thought afar off.

You comprehend my path and my lying down,

And are acquainted with all my ways.

For there is not a word on my tongue,

But behold, O LORD, You know it altogether.

PSALM 139:1-4 NKJV

S	M	T	W	T	F	S
						1
2	3	4	5	6	7	8
9	10	11	12	13	14	15
16	17	18	19	20	21	22
23	24	25	26	27	28	29
30	31					

December

3 Monday

_____
_____
_____
_____

4 Tuesday

_____
_____
_____
_____

5 Wednesday

_____
_____
_____
_____
_____

Thursday 6

_____
_____
_____
_____
_____

Friday 7

_____
_____
_____
_____

Saturday 8

_____
_____
_____

Sunday 9

_____
_____
_____

THE LORD GIVES WISDOM;
FROM HIS MOUTH COME KNOWLEDGE AND UNDERSTANDING.

Proverbs 2:6-7 ESV

December

10 Monday   HANUKKAH ENDS

_____
_____
_____
_____

11 Tuesday

_____
_____
_____
_____

12 Wednesday

_____
_____
_____
_____

Thursday 13

Friday 14

Saturday 15

Sunday 16

THE WISDOM FROM ABOVE IS FIRST OF ALL PURE.
IT IS ALSO PEACE LOVING, GENTLE AT ALL TIMES,
AND WILLING TO YIELD TO OTHERS.
IT IS FULL OF MERCY AND GOOD DEEDS.
IT SHOWS NO FAVORITISM AND IS ALWAYS SINCERE.

James 3:17 NLT

December

17 Monday

_____
_____
_____
_____

18 Tuesday

_____
_____
_____
_____

19 Wednesday

_____
_____
_____
_____
_____

Thursday 20

WINTER SOLSTICE Friday 21

Saturday 22

Sunday 23

YOU WILL EXPERIENCE GOD'S PEACE,
WHICH EXCEEDS ANYTHING WE CAN UNDERSTAND.
HIS PEACE WILL GUARD YOUR HEARTS AND MINDS
AS YOU LIVE IN CHRIST JESUS.

Philippians 4:7 NLT

December

24 Monday CHRISTMAS EVE

_____
_____
_____
_____
_____

25 Tuesday CHRISTMAS DAY

_____
_____
_____
_____
_____

26 Wednesday

_____
_____
_____
_____
_____

Thursday 27

Friday 28

Saturday 29

Sunday 30

HE WHO HAS CLEAN HANDS AND A PURE HEART,
WHO HAS NOT LIFTED UP HIS SOUL TO FALSEHOOD
AND HAS NOT SWORN DECEITFULLY.
HE SHALL RECEIVE A BLESSING FROM THE LORD
AND RIGHTEOUSNESS FROM THE GOD OF HIS SALVATION.

Psalm 24:5 NASB

January

2019

God has said,

"I will never fail you.

I will never abandon you."

So we can say with confidence,

"The LORD is my helper,

so I will have no fear."

HEBREWS 13:5-6 NLT

S	M	T	W	T	F	S
		1	2	3	4	5
6	7	8	9	10	11	12
13	14	15	16	17	18	19
20	21	22	23	24	25	26
27	28	29	30	31		

December/January

31 Monday   NEW YEAR'S EVE

_____
_____
_____
_____

1 Tuesday   NEW YEAR'S DAY

_____
_____
_____
_____

2 Wednesday

_____
_____
_____
_____
_____

Thursday 3

Friday 4

Saturday 5

Sunday 6

THE LORD LOVES JUSTICE AND FAIRNESS;
HE WILL NEVER ABANDON HIS PEOPLE.
THEY WILL BE KEPT SAFE FOREVER.

Psalm 37:28 TLB

January

7   Monday

_____
_____
_____
_____
_____

8   Tuesday

_____
_____
_____
_____
_____

9   Wednesday

_____
_____
_____
_____
_____

Thursday 10

Friday 11

Saturday 12

Sunday 13

THE LORD HEARS HIS PEOPLE WHEN THEY CALL TO HIM FOR HELP.
HE RESCUES THEM FROM ALL THEIR TROUBLES.

Psalm 34:17 NLT

January

14 Monday

_____
_____
_____
_____
_____

15 Tuesday

_____
_____
_____
_____
_____

16 Wednesday

_____
_____
_____
_____
_____

Thursday 17

Friday 18

Saturday 19

Sunday 20

IF GOD IS FOR US, WHO CAN BE AGAINST US?

Romans 8:31 ESV

January

21 Monday   MARTIN LUTHER KING JR. DAY

_____
_____
_____
_____
_____

22 Tuesday

_____
_____
_____
_____
_____

23 Wednesday

_____
_____
_____
_____
_____

Thursday 24

_____
_____
_____
_____
_____

Friday 25

_____
_____
_____
_____
_____

Saturday 26

_____
_____
_____

Sunday 27

_____
_____
_____

SUBMIT TO GOD. RESIST THE DEVIL AND HE WILL FLEE FROM YOU.

James 4:7 NKJV

February

2019

Take delight in the LORD,

and he will give you your heart's desires.

Commit everything you do to the LORD.

Trust him, and he will help you.

PSALM 37:4-5 NLT

S	M	T	W	T	F	S
					1	2
3	4	5	6	7	8	9
10	11	12	13	14	15	16
17	18	19	20	21	22	23
24	25	26	27	28		

January/February

28 Monday

_____
_____
_____
_____
_____

29 Tuesday

_____
_____
_____
_____
_____

30 Wednesday

_____
_____
_____
_____
_____

_____
_____
_____
_____
_____

Friday 1

_____
_____
_____
_____

Saturday 2

_____
_____

Sunday 3

_____
_____
_____

THOSE WITH GOOD SENSE ARE SLOW TO ANGER,
AND IT IS THEIR GLORY TO OVERLOOK AN OFFENSE.

Proverbs 19:11 NRSV

February

4 Monday

_____
_____
_____
_____
_____

5 Tuesday

_____
_____
_____
_____
_____

6 Wednesday

_____
_____
_____
_____
_____

Thursday 7

Friday 8

Saturday 9

Sunday 10

YOU KEEP HIM IN PERFECT PEACE
WHOSE MIND IS STAYED ON YOU,
BECAUSE HE TRUSTS IN YOU.

Isaiah 26:3 ESV

February

11 Monday

_____

_____

_____

_____

_____

12 Tuesday

_____

_____

_____

_____

_____

13 Wednesday

_____

_____

_____

_____

_____

_____
_____
_____
_____
_____

Friday 15

_____
_____
_____
_____

Saturday 16

_____
_____

Sunday 17

_____
_____
_____

"BLESSED ARE THOSE WHO HAVE NOT SEEN AND YET HAVE BELIEVED."

John 20:29 ESV

February

18 Monday   PRESIDENTS' DAY

_____
_____
_____
_____
_____

19 Tuesday

_____
_____
_____
_____
_____

20 Wednesday

_____
_____
_____
_____
_____

Thursday 21

Friday 22

Saturday 23

Sunday 24

Surely you have granted him unending blessings
and made him glad with the joy of your presence.

Psalm 21:6 NIV

February / March

25 Monday

_____
_____
_____
_____
_____

26 Tuesday

_____
_____
_____
_____
_____

27 Wednesday

_____
_____
_____
_____
_____

_____
_____
_____
_____
_____

Friday 1

_____
_____
_____
_____

Saturday 2

_____
_____
_____

Sunday 3

_____
_____
_____

RELIGION THAT IS PURE AND UNDEFILED BEFORE GOD,
THE FATHER, IS THIS: TO CARE FOR ORPHANS AND WIDOWS IN
THEIR DISTRESS, AND TO KEEP ONESELF UNSTAINED BY THE WORLD.

James 1:27 NRSV

March

2019

Blessed be the God and Father of our Lord Jesus Christ, who has blessed us in Christ with every spiritual blessing in the heavenly places, even as he chose us in him before the foundation of the world, that we should be holy and blameless before him.

EPHESIANS 1:3-4 ESV

S	M	T	W	T	F	S
					1	2
3	4	5	6	7	8	9
10	11	12	13	14	15	16
17	18	19	20	21	22	23
24	25	26	27	28	29	30
31						

March

4   Monday

_____
_____
_____
_____
_____

5   Tuesday

_____
_____
_____
_____
_____

6   Wednesday   ASH WEDNESDAY

_____
_____
_____
_____
_____

Thursday 7

Friday 8

Saturday 9

Sunday 10

EVERY GOOD GIFT AND EVERY PERFECT GIFT IS FROM ABOVE,
COMING DOWN FROM THE FATHER OF LIGHTS WITH WHOM THERE
IS NO VARIATION OR SHADOW DUE TO CHANGE.

James 1:17 ESV

March

11 Monday

_____
_____
_____
_____

12 Tuesday

_____
_____
_____
_____

13 Wednesday

_____
_____
_____
_____

Thursday 14

Friday 15

Saturday 16

Sunday 17

"SEEK FIRST THE KINGDOM OF GOD AND HIS RIGHTEOUSNESS,
AND ALL THESE THINGS SHALL BE ADDED TO YOU."

Matthew 6:33 NKJV

March

18 Monday

_____
_____
_____
_____

19 Tuesday

_____
_____
_____
_____

20 Wednesday   SPRING EQUINOX

_____
_____
_____
_____
_____

Thursday 21

Friday 22

Saturday 23

Sunday 24

THE LORD LONGS TO BE GRACIOUS TO YOU;
THEREFORE HE WILL RISE UP TO SHOW YOU COMPASSION.
FOR THE LORD IS A GOD OF JUSTICE.
BLESSED ARE ALL WHO WAIT FOR HIM!

Isaiah 30:18 NIV

March

25 Monday

_____
_____
_____
_____

26 Tuesday

_____
_____
_____
_____

27 Wednesday

_____
_____
_____
_____
_____

Thursday 28

_____
_____
_____
_____
_____

Friday 29

_____
_____
_____
_____
_____

Saturday 30

_____
_____
_____

Sunday 31

_____
_____
_____

I CAN DO EVERYTHING THROUGH CHRIST, WHO GIVES ME STRENGTH.

Philippians 4:13 NLT

April
2019

I will sing of the LORD's great love forever;

with my mouth I will make your faithfulness

known through all generations.

I will declare that your

love stands firm forever,

that you have established

your faithfulness in heaven itself.

PSALM 89:1-2 NIV

S	M	T	W	T	F	S
	1	2	3	4	5	6
7	8	9	10	11	12	13
14	15	16	17	18	19	20
21	22	23	24	25	26	27
28	29	30				

April

1   Monday

_____
_____
_____
_____

2   Tuesday

_____
_____
_____
_____

3   Wednesday

_____
_____
_____
_____
_____

Thursday 4

Friday 5

Saturday 6

Sunday

LET US THEN APPROACH GOD'S THRONE OF GRACE
WITH CONFIDENCE, SO THAT WE MAY RECEIVE MERCY
AND FIND GRACE TO HELP US IN OUR TIME OF NEED.

Hebrews 4:16 NIV

April

8   Monday

_____
_____
_____
_____
_____

9   Tuesday

_____
_____
_____
_____
_____

10   Wednesday

_____
_____
_____
_____
_____

Thursday 11

Friday 12

Saturday 13

Sunday 14

WE ARE GOD'S MASTERPIECE. HE HAS CREATED US
ANEW IN CHRIST JESUS, SO WE CAN DO THE GOOD
THINGS HE PLANNED FOR US LONG AGO.

Ephesians 2:10 NLT

April

15 Monday

_____
_____
_____
_____
_____

16 Tuesday

_____
_____
_____
_____
_____

17 Wednesday

_____
_____
_____
_____
_____

BE OF THE SAME MIND TOWARD ONE ANOTHER. DO NOT
SET YOUR MIND ON HIGH THINGS, BUT ASSOCIATE WITH
THE HUMBLE. DO NOT BE WISE IN YOUR OWN OPINION.

Romans 12:16 NKJV

April

22 Monday

_____
_____
_____
_____
_____

23 Tuesday

_____
_____
_____
_____
_____

24 Wednesday

_____
_____
_____
_____
_____

Thursday 25

Friday 26

Saturday 27

Sunday 28

BE STRONG AND COURAGEOUS. DO NOT BE
FRIGHTENED, AND DO NOT BE DISMAYED, FOR THE
LORD YOUR GOD IS WITH YOU WHEREVER YOU GO.

Joshua 1:9 ESV

May

2019

Be my rock of refuge,

to which I can always go;

give the command to save me,

for you are my rock and my fortress....

You have been my hope, Sovereign LORD,

my confidence since my youth.

PSALM 71:3, 5 NIV

S	M	T	W	T	F	S
			1	2	3	4
5	6	7	8	9	10	11
12	13	14	15	16	17	18
19	20	21	22	23	24	25
26	27	28	29	30	31	

April/May

29 Monday

_____
_____
_____
_____
_____

30 Tuesday

_____
_____
_____
_____
_____

1 Wednesday

_____
_____
_____
_____
_____

_____
_____
_____
_____
_____

Friday 3

_____
_____
_____
_____

Saturday 4

_____
_____
_____

Sunday 5

_____
_____
_____

THE WHOLE EARTH IS FILLED WITH AWE AT YOUR WONDERS.

Psalm 65:8 NIV

May

6   Monday

_____
_____
_____
_____
_____

7   Tuesday

_____
_____
_____
_____
_____

8   Wednesday

_____
_____
_____
_____
_____

Thursday 9

_____
_____
_____
_____
_____

Friday 10

_____
_____
_____
_____
_____

Saturday 11

_____
_____
_____

_____
_____
_____

WHY AM I SO SAD?
WHY AM I SO UPSET?
I SHOULD PUT MY HOPE IN GOD
AND KEEP PRAISING HIM.

Psalm 42:11 NCV

May

13 Monday

_____
_____
_____
_____
_____

14 Tuesday

_____
_____
_____
_____
_____

15 Wednesday

_____
_____
_____
_____

Thursday 16

_____
_____
_____
_____
_____

Friday 17

_____
_____
_____
_____
_____

Saturday 18

_____
_____
_____

Sunday 19

_____
_____
_____

TAKE A NEW GRIP WITH YOUR TIRED HANDS AND STRENGTHEN YOUR
WEAK KNEES. MARK OUT A STRAIGHT PATH FOR YOUR FEET SO THAT
THOSE WHO ARE WEAK AND LAME WILL NOT FALL BUT BECOME STRONG.

Hebrews 12:12-14 NLT

May

20 Monday

_____
_____
_____
_____

21 Tuesday

_____
_____
_____
_____

22 Wednesday

_____
_____
_____
_____
_____

Thursday 23

Friday 24

Saturday 25

Sunday 26

WHOEVER PURSUES RIGHTEOUSNESS AND LOVE FINDS LIFE,
PROSPERITY AND HONOR.

Proverbs 21:21 NIV

May / June

27 Monday   MEMORIAL DAY

_____
_____
_____
_____
_____

28 Tuesday

_____
_____
_____
_____
_____

29 Wednesday

_____
_____
_____
_____
_____

Thursday 30

Friday 31

Saturday 1

Sunday 2

LET US NOT NEGLECT OUR MEETING TOGETHER, AS SOME
PEOPLE DO, BUT ENCOURAGE ONE ANOTHER, ESPECIALLY
NOW THAT THE DAY OF HIS RETURN IS DRAWING NEAR.

Hebrews 10:25 NLT

June

2019

The Lord your God is in your midst,

a mighty one who will save;

he will rejoice over you with gladness;

he will quiet you by his love;

he will exult over you with loud singing.

ZEPHANIAH 3:17 ESV

S	M	T	W	T	F	S
						1
2	3	4	5	6	7	8
9	10	11	12	13	14	15
16	17	18	19	20	21	22
23	24	25	26	27	28	29
30						

June

3 Monday

_____
_____
_____
_____

4 Tuesday

_____
_____
_____
_____

5 Wednesday

_____
_____
_____
_____

Thursday 6

Friday 7

Saturday 8

Sunday 9

Do your best to present yourself to God as one
approved by him, a worker who has no need to be
ashamed, rightly explaining the word of truth.

2 Timothy 2:15 NRSV

June

10 Monday

_____
_____
_____
_____
_____

11 Tuesday

_____
_____
_____
_____
_____

12 Wednesday

_____
_____
_____
_____
_____

Friday 14

Saturday 15

FATHER'S DAY Sunday 16

"I WILL COME BACK AND TAKE YOU TO BE WITH
ME THAT YOU ALSO MAY BE WHERE I AM."

John 14:3 NIV

June

17 Monday

_____
_____
_____
_____
_____

18 Tuesday

_____
_____
_____
_____
_____

19 Wednesday

_____
_____
_____
_____
_____

Thursday 20

SUMMER SOLSTICE Friday 21

Saturday 22

Sunday 23

"IF YOU HAVE FAITH LIKE A GRAIN OF MUSTARD SEED, YOU WILL SAY
TO THIS MOUNTAIN, 'MOVE FROM HERE TO THERE,' AND IT WILL
MOVE, AND NOTHING WILL BE IMPOSSIBLE FOR YOU."

Matthew 17:20 ESV

June

24 Monday

_____
_____
_____
_____
_____

25 Tuesday

_____
_____
_____
_____
_____

26 Wednesday

_____
_____
_____
_____
_____

Thursday 27

_____

_____

_____

_____

_____

Friday 28

_____

_____

_____

_____

_____

Saturday 29

_____

_____

_____

Sunday 30

_____

_____

_____

WHETHER YOU EAT OR DRINK,
OR WHATEVER YOU DO, DO ALL TO THE GLORY OF GOD.

1 Corinthians 10:31 NKJV

July

2019

You created my inmost being;

you knit me together in my mother's womb.

I praise you because I am fearfully

and wonderfully made;

your works are wonderful,

I know that full well.

PSALM 139:13-14 NIV

S	M	T	W	T	F	S
	1	2	3	4	5	6
7	8	9	10	11	12	13
14	15	16	17	18	19	20
21	22	23	24	25	26	27
28	29	30	31			

July

1 Monday

_____
_____
_____
_____

2 Tuesday

_____
_____
_____
_____

3 Wednesday

_____
_____
_____
_____
_____

Friday 5

Saturday 6

Sunday 7

WITHOUT FAITH IT IS IMPOSSIBLE TO PLEASE GOD, BECAUSE
ANYONE WHO COMES TO HIM MUST BELIEVE THAT HE EXISTS
AND THAT HE REWARDS THOSE WHO EARNESTLY SEEK HIM.

Hebrews 11:6 NIV

July

8 Monday

_____

_____

_____

_____

_____

9 Tuesday

_____

_____

_____

_____

_____

10 Wednesday

_____

_____

_____

_____

_____

_____
_____
_____
_____

Friday 12

_____
_____
_____
_____

Saturday 13

_____
_____

Sunday 14

_____
_____
_____

GOD IS FAITHFUL. HE WILL NOT ALLOW THE
TEMPTATION TO BE MORE THAN YOU CAN STAND.
WHEN YOU ARE TEMPTED, HE WILL SHOW YOU A WAY
OUT SO THAT YOU CAN ENDURE.

1 Corinthians 10:13 NLT

July

15 Monday

_____
_____
_____
_____
_____

16 Tuesday

_____
_____
_____
_____
_____

17 Wednesday

_____
_____
_____
_____
_____

_____
_____
_____
_____
_____

Friday 19

_____
_____
_____
_____

Saturday 20

_____
_____

Sunday 21

_____
_____
_____

WHEN YOU LIE DOWN,
YOU WILL NOT BE AFRAID;
WHEN YOU LIE DOWN,
YOUR SLEEP WILL BE SWEET.

Proverbs 3:24 NIV

July

22 Monday

_____
_____
_____
_____

23 Tuesday

_____
_____
_____
_____

24 Wednesday

_____
_____
_____
_____
_____

Thursday 25

Friday 26

Saturday 27

Sunday 28

GOD HAS NOT GIVEN US A SPIRIT OF FEAR,
BUT OF POWER AND OF LOVE AND OF A SOUND MIND.

2 Timothy 1:7 NKJV

August
2019

Consider it pure joy, my brothers and sisters, whenever you face trials of many kinds, because you know that the testing of your faith produces perseverance.

JAMES 1:2-3 NIV

	S	M	T	W	T	F	S
					1	2	3
	4	5	6	7	8	9	10
	11	12	13	14	15	16	17
	18	19	20	21	22	23	24
	25	26	27	28	29	30	31

July / August

29 Monday

_____
_____
_____
_____
_____

30 Tuesday

_____
_____
_____
_____
_____

31 Wednesday

_____
_____
_____
_____
_____

Thursday 1

_____

Friday 2

_____

Saturday 3

_____

Sunday 4

_____

YOU ARE OUR FATHER;
WE ARE THE CLAY, AND YOU OUR POTTER;
AND ALL WE ARE THE WORK OF YOUR HAND.

Isaiah 64:8 NKJV

August

5   Monday

_____
_____
_____
_____

6   Tuesday

_____
_____
_____
_____

7   Wednesday

_____
_____
_____
_____

Thursday 8

Friday 9

Saturday 10

Sunday 11

He is so rich in kindness and grace that
he purchased our freedom with the
blood of his Son and forgave our sins.

Ephesians 1:7 NLT

August

12 Monday

_____
_____
_____
_____
_____

13 Tuesday

_____
_____
_____
_____
_____

14 Wednesday

_____
_____
_____
_____
_____

Thursday 15

_____
_____
_____
_____
_____

Friday 16

_____
_____
_____
_____
_____

Saturday 17

_____
_____
_____

Sunday 18

_____
_____
_____

You, Lord, are good, and ready to forgive,
And abundant in mercy to all those who call upon You.

Psalm 86:5 NKJV

August

19 Monday

_____
_____
_____
_____
_____

20 Tuesday

_____
_____
_____
_____
_____

21 Wednesday

_____
_____
_____
_____
_____

Thursday 22

Friday 23

Saturday 24

Sunday 25

Whoever is generous to the poor lends to the Lord,
and he will repay him for his deed.

Proverbs 19:17 ESV

August/September

26 Monday

_____
_____
_____
_____
_____
_____

27 Tuesday

_____
_____
_____
_____
_____

28 Wednesday

_____
_____
_____
_____
_____

Thursday 29

_____
_____
_____
_____
_____

Friday 30

_____
_____
_____
_____

Saturday 31

_____
_____
_____

Sunday 1

_____
_____
_____

"BLESSED ARE THE GENTLE, FOR THEY SHALL INHERIT THE EARTH."

Matthew 5:5 NASB

September
2019

We do not lose heart, but though our outer man is decaying, yet our inner man is being renewed day by day. For momentary, light affliction is producing for us an eternal weight of glory far beyond all comparison.

2 CORINTHIANS 4:16-17 NASB

S	M	T	W	T	F	S
1	2	3	4	5	6	7
8	9	10	11	12	13	14
15	16	17	18	19	20	21
22	23	24	25	26	27	28
29	30					

September

2 Monday LABOR DAY

_____
_____
_____
_____
_____

3 Tuesday

_____
_____
_____
_____
_____

4 Wednesday

_____
_____
_____
_____
_____

Thursday 5

Friday 6

Saturday 7

Sunday 8

THE LORD IS GOOD TO ALL,
AND HIS MERCY IS OVER ALL THAT HE HAS MADE.

Psalm 145:9 ESV

September

9   Monday

_____
_____
_____
_____
_____

10 Tuesday

_____
_____
_____
_____
_____

11 Wednesday

_____
_____
_____
_____
_____

Thursday 12

_____
_____
_____
_____
_____

Friday 13

_____
_____
_____
_____
_____

Saturday 14

_____
_____
_____

Sunday 15

_____
_____
_____

THE RANSOMED OF THE LORD WILL RETURN. THEY WILL
ENTER ZION WITH SINGING; EVERLASTING JOY WILL CROWN
THEIR HEADS. GLADNESS AND JOY WILL OVERTAKE THEM,
AND SORROW AND SIGHING WILL FLEE AWAY.

Isaiah 35:10 NIV

September

16 Monday

_____
_____
_____
_____

17 Tuesday

_____
_____
_____
_____

18 Wednesday

_____
_____
_____
_____
_____

Friday 20

Saturday 21

Sunday 22

I CONSIDER THAT THE SUFFERINGS OF THIS PRESENT TIME ARE NOT
WORTH COMPARING WITH THE GLORY THAT IS TO BE REVEALED TO US.

Romans 8:18 ESV

September

23 Monday   AUTUMNAL EQUINOX

_____
_____
_____
_____
_____

24 Tuesday

_____
_____
_____
_____
_____

25 Wednesday

_____
_____
_____
_____
_____

Thursday 26

Friday 27

Saturday 28

Sunday 29

WE CAN MAKE OUR PLANS, BUT THE LORD DETERMINES OUR STEPS.

Proverbs 16:9 NLT

October
2019

With me are riches and honor,

enduring wealth and prosperity.

My fruit is better than fine gold;

what I yield surpasses choice silver.

I walk in the way of righteousness,

along the paths of justice,

bestowing a rich inheritance

on those who love me

and making their treasuries full.

PROVERBS 8:18-21 NIV

S	M	T	W	T	F	S
		1	2	3	4	5
6	7	8	9	10	11	12
13	14	15	16	17	18	19
20	21	22	23	24	25	26
27	28	29	30	31		

September/October

30 Monday ROSH HASHANAH

_____
_____
_____
_____
_____

1 Tuesday

_____
_____
_____
_____
_____

2 Wednesday

_____
_____
_____
_____
_____

Thursday 3

_____
_____
_____
_____
_____

Friday 4

_____
_____
_____
_____
_____

Saturday 5

_____
_____
_____

Sunday 6

_____
_____
_____

THOSE WHO DEAL TRUTHFULLY ARE HIS DELIGHT.

Proverbs 12:22 NKJV

October

7   Monday

_____
_____
_____
_____
_____

8   Tuesday   YOM KIPPUR

_____
_____
_____
_____
_____

9   Wednesday

_____
_____
_____
_____
_____

Thursday 10

Friday 11

Saturday 12

Sunday 13

"MY FATHER WILL HONOR THE ONE WHO SERVES ME."

John 12:26 NIV

October

14 Monday COLUMBUS DAY

_____
_____
_____
_____

15 Tuesday

_____
_____
_____
_____

16 Wednesday

_____
_____
_____
_____

Thursday 17

_____
_____
_____
_____
_____

Friday 18

_____
_____
_____
_____
_____

Saturday 19

_____
_____
_____

Sunday 20

_____
_____
_____
_____

THE LORD TAKES PLEASURE IN THOSE WHO FEAR HIM,
IN THOSE WHO HOPE IN HIS MERCY.

Psalm 147:11 NKJV

October

21 Monday

_____
_____
_____
_____
_____

22 Tuesday

_____
_____
_____
_____
_____

23 Wednesday

_____
_____
_____
_____
_____

Friday 25

Saturday 26

Sunday 27

PRIDE WILL RUIN PEOPLE,
BUT THOSE WHO ARE HUMBLE WILL BE HONORED.

Proverbs 29:23 NCV

November
2019

My child, pay attention to what I say.

Listen carefully to my words.

Don't lose sight of them.

Let them penetrate deep into your heart,

for they bring life to those who find them,

and healing to their whole body.

PROVERBS 4:20-22 NLT

S	M	T	W	T	F	S
					1	2
3	4	5	6	7	8	9
10	11	12	13	14	15	16
17	18	19	20	21	22	23
24	25	26	27	28	29	30

October/November

28 Monday

_____
_____
_____
_____

29 Tuesday

_____
_____
_____
_____

30 Wednesday

_____
_____
_____
_____

Thursday 31

Friday 1

Saturday 2

DAYLIGHT SAVING TIME ENDS Sunday 3

YOUR LAWS ARE MY TREASURE;
THEY ARE MY HEART'S DELIGHT.

Psalm 119:111 NLT

November

4   Monday

_____
_____
_____
_____
_____

5   Tuesday

_____
_____
_____
_____
_____

6   Wednesday

_____
_____
_____
_____
_____

Thursday   7

_____
_____
_____
_____
_____

Friday   8

_____
_____
_____
_____

Saturday   9

_____
_____
_____

Sunday   10

_____
_____
_____

BECAUSE OF MY INTEGRITY YOU UPHOLD ME
AND SET ME IN YOUR PRESENCE FOREVER.

Psalm 41:12 NIV

November

11 Monday   VETERANS' DAY

_____
_____
_____
_____
_____

12 Tuesday

_____
_____
_____
_____
_____

13 Wednesday

_____
_____
_____
_____
_____

Thursday 14

Friday 15

Saturday 16

Sunday 17

YOU WILL GO OUT WITH JOY AND BE LED OUT IN PEACE.
THE MOUNTAINS AND HILLS WILL BURST INTO SONG BEFORE YOU,
AND ALL THE TREES IN THE FIELDS WILL CLAP THEIR HANDS.

Isaiah 55:12 NCV

November

18 Monday

_____
_____
_____
_____
_____

19 Tuesday

_____
_____
_____
_____
_____

20 Wednesday

_____
_____
_____
_____
_____

Thursday 21

Friday 22

Saturday 23

Sunday 24

Righteousness and justice are
the foundation of your throne.

Psalm 89:14 NIV

November/December

25 Monday

_____
_____
_____
_____
_____

26 Tuesday

_____
_____
_____
_____
_____

27 Wednesday

_____
_____
_____
_____
_____

_____
_____
_____
_____
_____

Friday 29

_____
_____
_____
_____

Saturday 30

_____
_____
_____

FIRST SUNDAY OF ADVENT Sunday 1

_____
_____
_____

THE LORD IS COMING TO JUDGE THE EARTH.
HE WILL JUDGE THE WORLD WITH JUSTICE,
AND THE NATIONS WITH FAIRNESS.

Psalm 98:9 NLT

December
2019

"You are the light of the world. A city set on a hill cannot be hidden. Nor do people light a lamp and put it under a basket, but on a stand, and it gives light to all in the house. In the same way, let your light shine before others, so that they may see your good works and give glory to your Father who is in heaven."

MATTHEW 5:14-16 ESV

	S	M	T	W	T	F	S
	1	2	3	4	5	6	7
	8	9	10	11	12	13	14
	15	16	17	18	19	20	21
	22	23	24	25	26	27	28
	29	30	31				

December

2 Monday

3 Tuesday

4 Wednesday

Thursday 5

_____

_____

_____

_____

Friday 6

_____

_____

_____

_____

Saturday 7

_____

_____

Sunday 8

_____

_____

_____

"LOVE YOUR ENEMIES, AND DO GOOD, AND LEND, EXPECTING
NOTHING IN RETURN, AND YOUR REWARD WILL BE GREAT,
AND YOU WILL BE SONS OF THE MOST HIGH."

Luke 6:35 ESV

December

9   Monday

_____
_____
_____
_____
_____

10   Tuesday

_____
_____
_____
_____
_____

11   Wednesday

_____
_____
_____
_____
_____

Thursday 12

Friday 13

Saturday 14

Sunday 15

Satisfy us in the morning with your unfailing love,
that we may sing for joy and be glad all our days.

Psalm 90:14 NIV

December

16 Monday

_____
_____
_____
_____
_____

17 Tuesday

_____
_____
_____
_____
_____

18 Wednesday

_____
_____
_____
_____
_____

Thursday 19

Friday 20

Saturday 21

WINTER SOLSTICE Sunday 22

THEY WHO WAIT FOR THE LORD SHALL RENEW THEIR
STRENGTH; THEY SHALL MOUNT UP WITH WINGS LIKE EAGLES;
THEY SHALL RUN AND NOT BE WEARY;
THEY SHALL WALK AND NOT FAINT.

Isaiah 40:31 ESV

December

23 Monday   HANUKKAH BEGINS

_____
_____
_____
_____
_____

24 Tuesday   CHRISTMAS EVE

_____
_____
_____
_____
_____

25 Wednesday   CHRISTMAS DAY

_____
_____
_____
_____
_____

Thursday 26

Friday 27

Saturday 28

Sunday 29

HANUKKAH ENDS Monday 30

NEW YEAR'S EVE Tuesday 31

Belle City Gifts
Savage, Minnesota, USA

Belle City Gifts is an imprint of BroadStreet Publishing Group LLC.
Broadstreetpublishing.com

Amazing Grace 2019 Planner

© 2018 by BroadStreet Publishing®

ISBN 978-1-4245-5693-9

Design by Garborg Design Works | garborgdesign.com
Compiled and edited by Michelle Winger | literallyprecise.com

Printed in China.